The
Zookeeper

by Lisa Olsson
illustrated by Carol Inouye

Scott Foresman

Editorial Offices: Glenview, Illinois • New York, New York
Sales Offices: Reading, Massachusetts • Duluth, Georgia
Glenview, Illinois • Carrollton, Texas • Menlo Park, California

I bring apples.

I hold one apple.

The elephant eats it.

The elephant wants more.

I bring fish.

I hold one fish.
The bear eats it.
The bear wants more.

I bring leaves.

I hold the leaves.

The giraffe eats them.

The giraffe wants more.

I bring carrots.

I hold the carrots.
The fox eats them.
The fox wants more.

I bring bananas.

I hold one banana.

The monkey eats it.

The monkey wants more.

I bring hay.

I hold the hay.
The zebra eats it.
The zebra wants more.

13

I bring milk.

I carry the fawn.
I hold the bottle.
The fawn is hungry.

I love my job!